THE BOOK OF TAKES

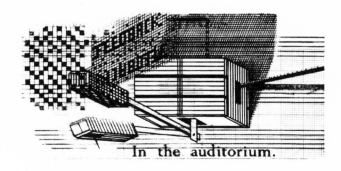

In the auditorium.

THE BOOK OF TAKES

PAUL ZELEVANSKY

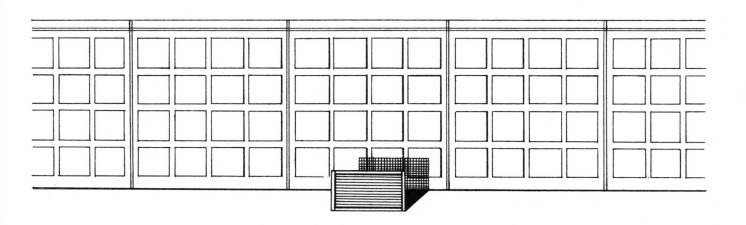

ZARTSCORP, INC. BOOKS, NEW YORK CITY, 1976

Library of Congress
Catalogue Card No.: 76-1809

PREFACE

THE BOOK OF TAKES is a personal account of the process of extracting art from life. The external storyline, the biography, is marked by the titles within the take signs. The nursery rhymes, songs, card games, etc., are metaphors for the experience of being. The central question is of the ever-present wall: What is it? How is it confronted? Does one overcome it?

THE BOOK OF TAKES is a chapter of a larger work called JERICHO. It is a book within a book. The form is new. The pictures are not appendages to, or illustrations of the words. The visual structure and the verbal structure are to be read together.

The book is most often read in columns, vertically, from page to page. It can also be read horizontally and, in the case of the card game, diagonally and in a circle. I would suggest that the reader let the work take him, at least on the first reading. Like all poetry, it is meant to be read many times. Pick sections out and savour them separately.

At the back of the book is the JERICHO map. At various points in the reading, you can locate yourself on it. It confirms the reader's physical existence inside the geography of JERICHO. This chapter takes place largely, but not exclusively, in the lower part of Sinai.

THE BOOK OF TAKES is highly condensed. It is constructed of the inter-relationships and reverberations of idea, language, space and time.

Lynn Hurwitz Zelevansky

GLOSSARY

Chairs, seats and vantage points.

Stairs, rivers and paths.

Tent, mountain, triangle.

Pole, cane, lever.

Top of the Wall.

The Wall; the page.

A camel who marks time.

A slow, lazy dog.

A quick, brown fox.

Rock, offspring, double.

Points of reference; blackboards.

EXTRACTS

The sign of simple activity. The efforts of mankind fill the space assigned to them, traversing it throughout.

The Book of Signs, Rudolf Koch.

Hebrew school primer.
(Copied by the author in 1958)

the geegees too, jesuistically formed at first but afterwards genuflected aggrily toewards the occident: the Ostrogothic kakography affected for certain phrases of Etruscan stabletalk and, in short, the learning betrayed at almost every line's end: the headstrength (at least eleven men of thirtytwo palfrycraft) revealed by a constant labour to make a ghimel pass through the eye of an iota: this, for instance, utterly unexpected sinistrogyric return to one peculiar sore point in the past; those throne open doubleyous (of an early muddy terranean origin whether man chooses to damn them agglutinatively loo — too — blue — face — ache or illvoodawpeehole or, kants koorts, topplefouls) seated with such

Finnegans Wake, James Joyce.

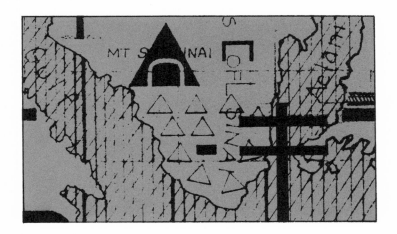

At Sinai, on the JERICHO map.

THE BOOK OF TAKES

Listening and Watching	Around the Wall	Approaching and Climbing
	below above	

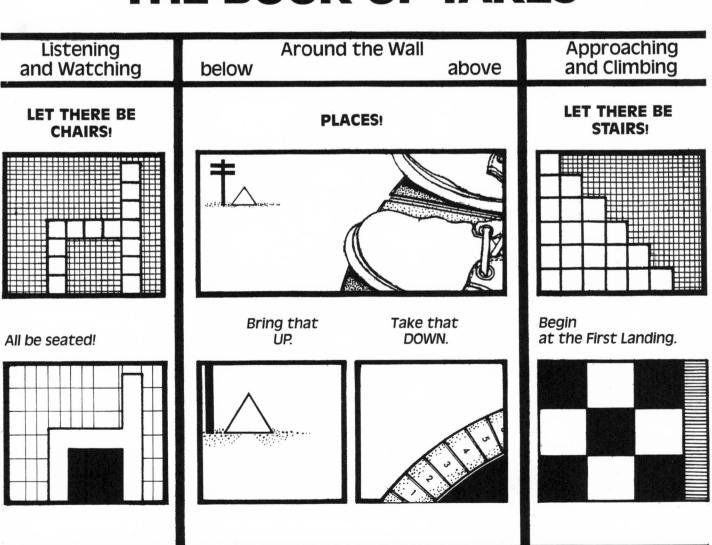

LET THERE BE CHAIRS!

PLACES!

LET THERE BE STAIRS!

All be seated!

Bring that UP.

Take that DOWN.

Begin at the First Landing.

Listening and Watching	Around the Wall		Approaching and Climbing
	below above		

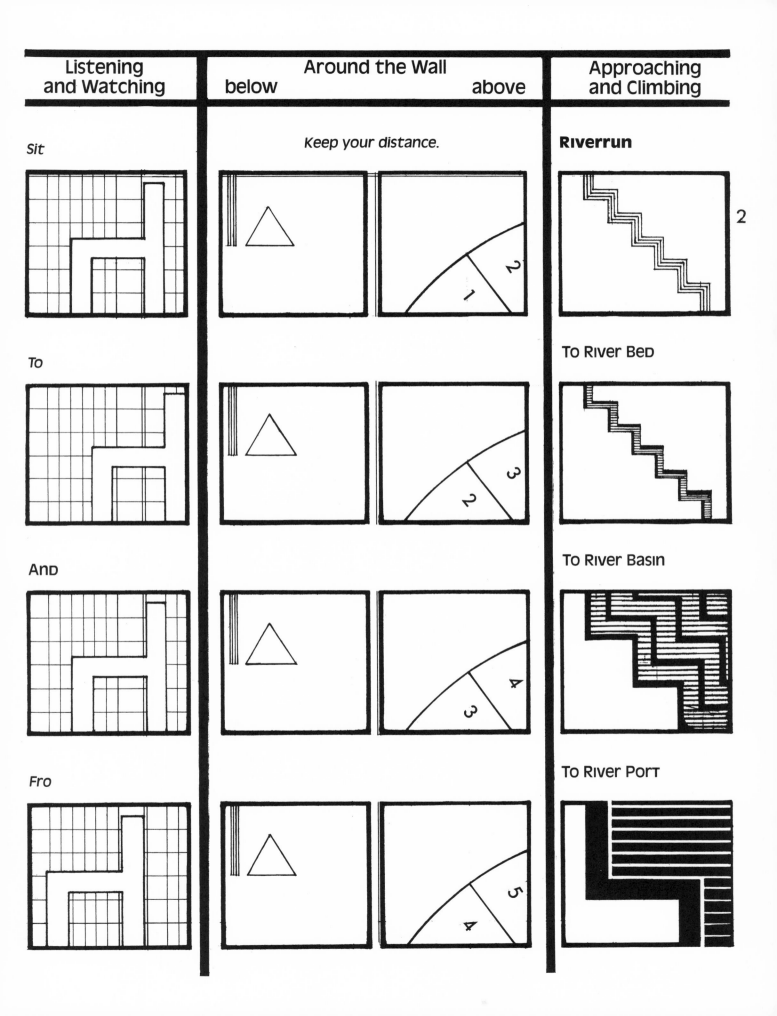

Listening and Watching

Sit

To

And

Fro

Around the Wall

below   above

Keep your distance.

Approaching and Climbing

Riverrun

2

To River Bed

To River Basin

To River Port

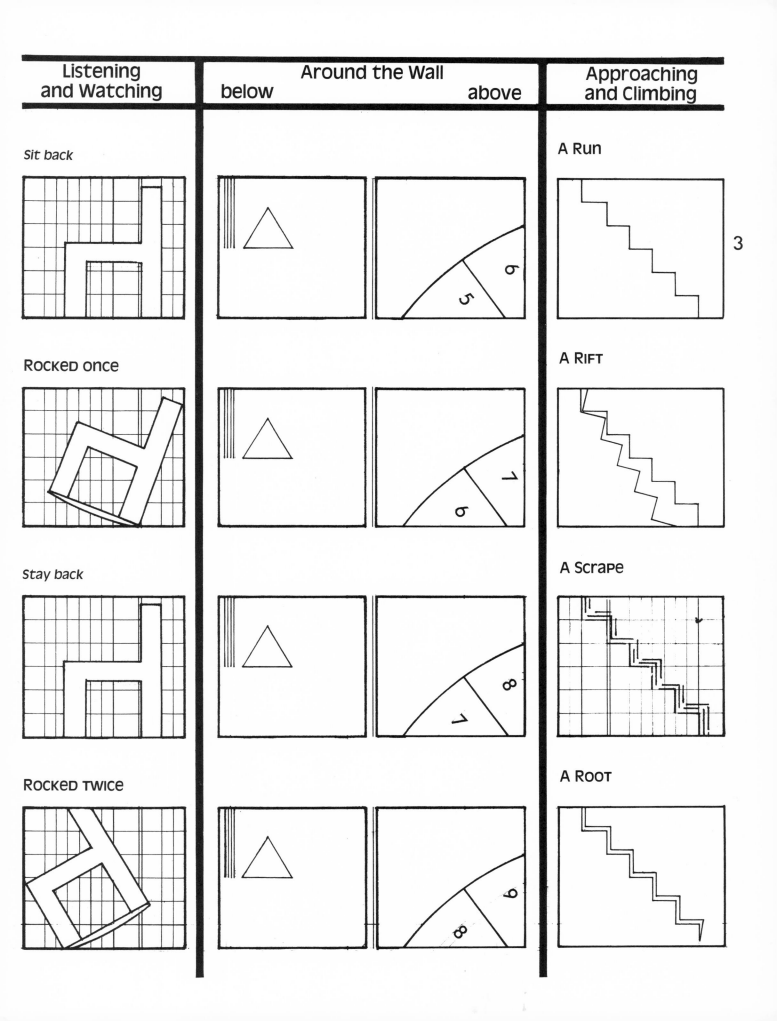

Listening and Watching	Around the Wall		Approaching and Climbing
	below	above	

Listening and Watching

Sit back

Rocked once

Stay back

Rocked twice

Around the Wall — below / above

Approaching and Climbing

A Run

A RIFT

A Scrape

A Root

3

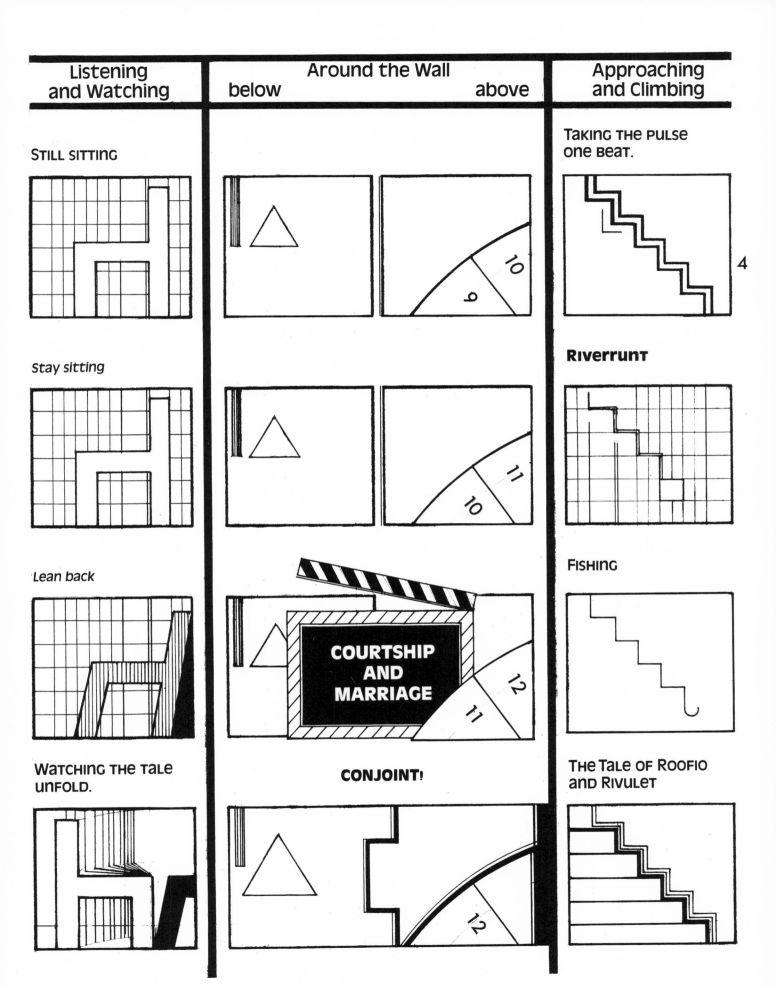

SITTING on the grass

HALF WITH HALF

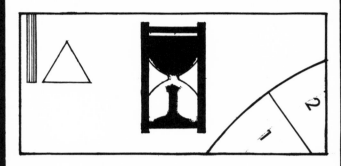

A HOLE IN ONE

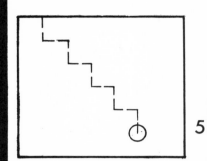

5

WATCHING from the wings

FAST WITH SLOW

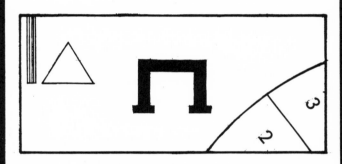

A PIROUETTE

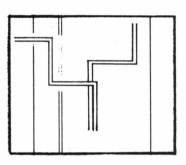

TILTING in the road

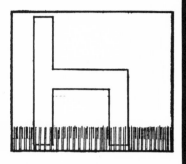

YES WITH NO

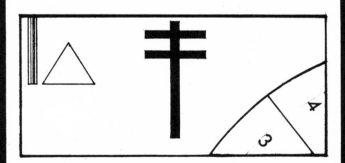

FROM ROCKFORD TO JOLIET

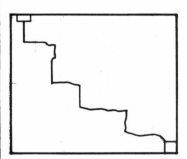

WAITING on the cliff

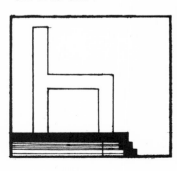

LATER TO MEET

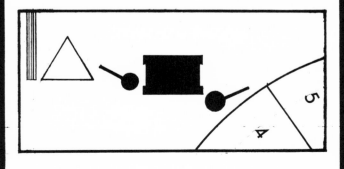

OVER THE FALLS

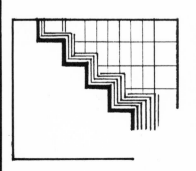

STACKED AND WAITING AT THE DAM

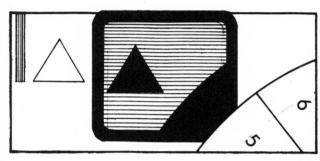

TO SPRING

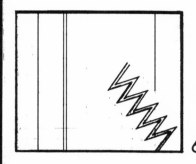

ALIGHTING FROM THE SECOND STORY

Ear say ye?

Say eye!

One DROP

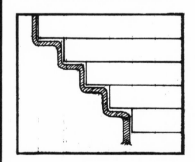

FOLDING ON THE DOTTED LINE

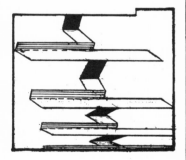

Out Of The Tent

TO CLOSE THE TALE OF ROPEO AND PARAPET

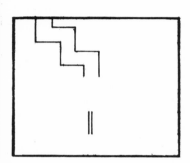

An EXIT LEFT

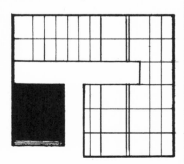

The First Audition
THE LOVER

*My love she is
A wand'ring bristle.
Her eyelids gListen,
She's no dumb person
Fair
(gEnough)*

FLUSH rIGHT

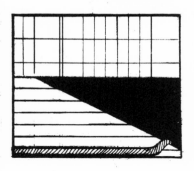

Out of the dark,
And into the open.

Out of the pause,
And into the former.

Out of the pane,
And into the mirror.

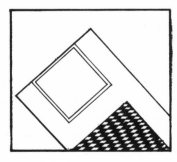

Out of the hall,
And into the foyer.

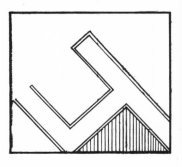

Go back in the tent!

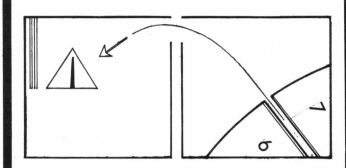

OF THE THIRD PERSON

muh muh muh muh muh muh muh muhmuh muh muh muh muh muh muh

INSTEP

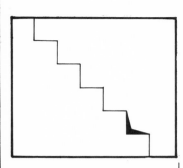

ONE STEP

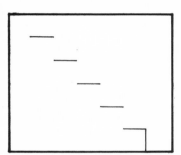

TWO STEP

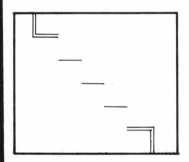

IN STEP

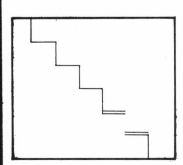

I see you

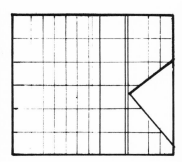

I see you

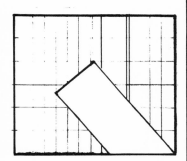

I see you

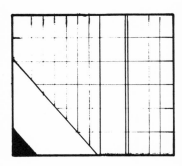

I see you

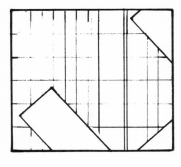

Furroway

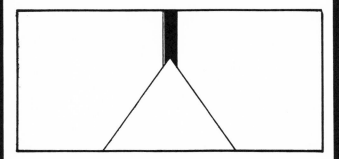

All be ceded!

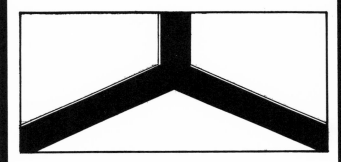

First Deal

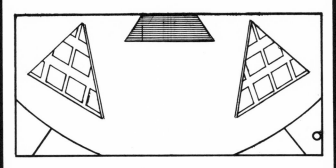

I'll see you yours, and raise you double.

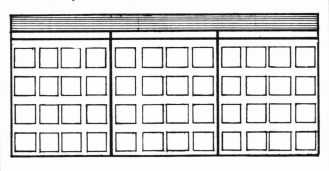

A STOOD, a STOOP

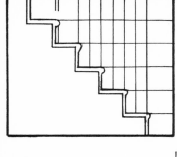

To STOOP, He, SHE, or IT STOOPS

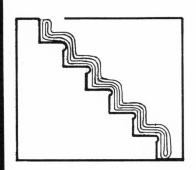

A ROUTE IN LOOP

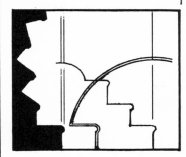

To SHOOT THE STALK

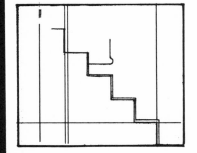

8

I see you

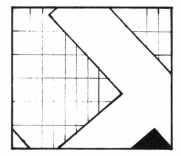

I'll take two,
and stand pat.

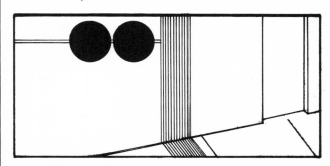

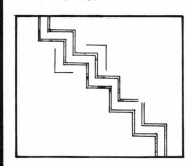

I see you

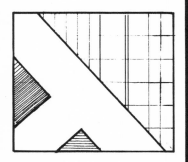

I'll pass and call
past port of call.

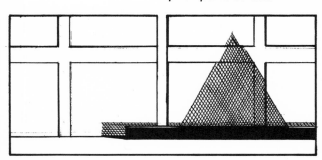

Riverrock

9

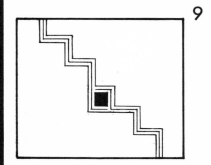

I see you

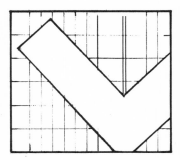

What's in your pocket,
a pair of eyes?

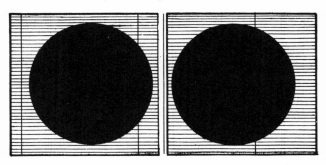

STEPPING OFF

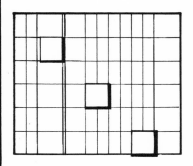

I see you

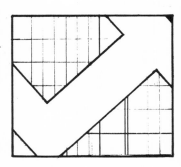

Who's there, Grandpa?

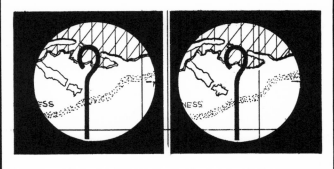

THE TALE OF CANE
AND ANTHILL

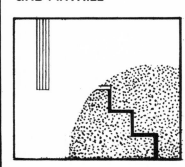

I see you

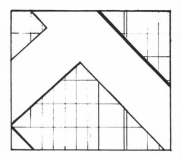

I'VE GOT YOU!

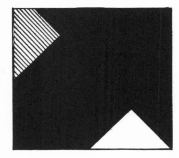

*I've got you
I've got you*

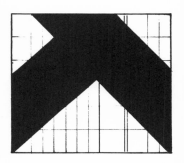

ALL MINE!

*See Saw
Close the door
All fall down!*

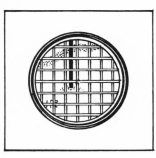 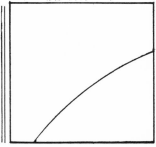

Past the mezzanine

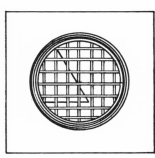 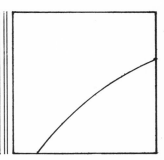

To the ground floor

 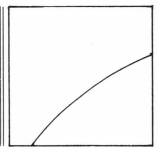

On the surface of things

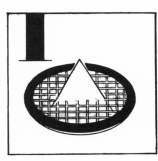 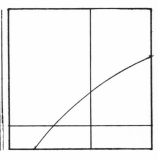

"AM I

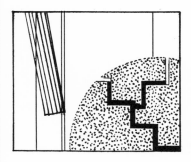

MY

10

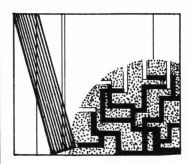

BROTHER'S

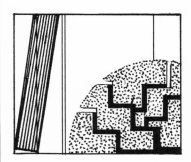

KEEPER?"

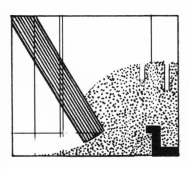

Beneath the Tree

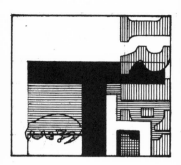

WITH FAMILY

To turn one THOUGHT
To mark one FLIGHT,
To leave one TRAIL
OF indenture.

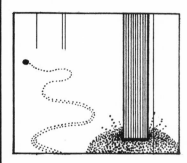

Your move

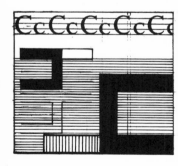

**The Second Audition
THE LONER**

*I've been a rambler
All my days.
I've lived on cornflakes
And mayonnaise.
With beer for breakfast
And donuts glazed
My eyes
For you.*

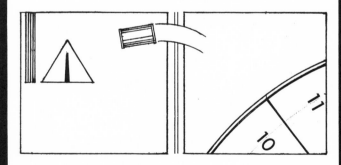

Bend

11

Undersea/Oversee

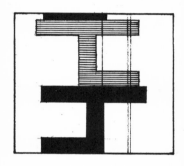

Go back in the tent!

A TRYSTING PATH

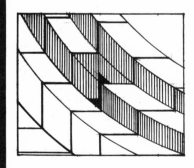

**History.
Early morning DUEL**

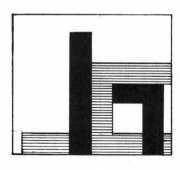

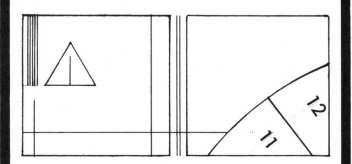

Past Carn and Arbor

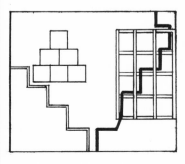

Hear 'O!
Hear 'O!

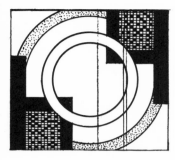

Glyphed

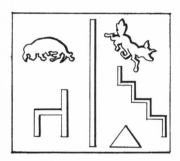

Marketing Stone

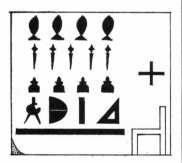

Tabular rising

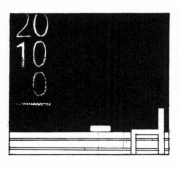

Citizen's Band

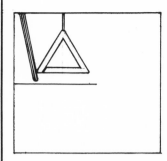
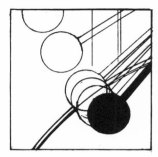

TAKE : A new setting.
The inkless channel
(The bloodless battle)

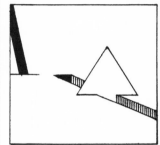

Inventory Wall:
Back to Book.

"Thou preparest a table..."

Can
My name is Able and
I come from Across
And my father aims
at Apples and

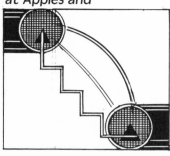

Stock Shift

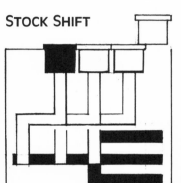

Filling in
Between arc and zero

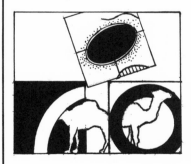

An early riser

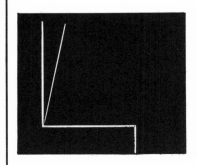

Grave Lines

Bench Scroll

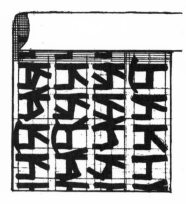

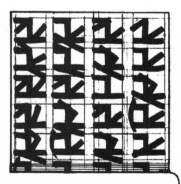

Council Footnote

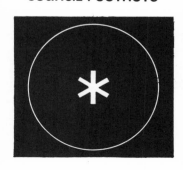

And rained at such intervals

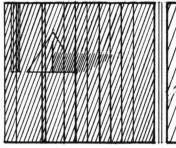
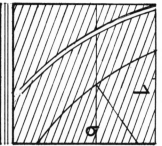

And rained at some intervals

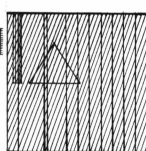
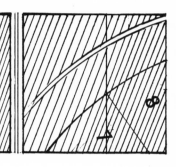

And rained at full intervals

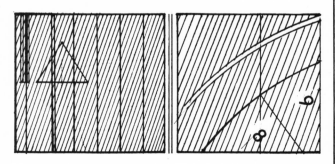

And watched the fire out.

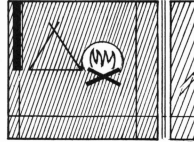

THE
Itsy-bitsy spider

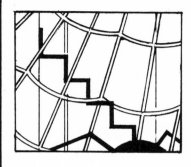

Climbed up
the water spout.

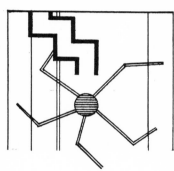

13

Down came the rain

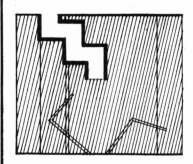

And washed
the spider out.

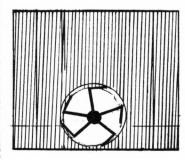

Let there be
The letter of the law.

ILLUMINATING LETTER

Ampersand

```
ᑫᑫᑫᑫᑫᑫᑫᑫᑫᑫᑫᑫᑫᑫᑫL
   THE BODY OF RA
ISED LITTERS HA
IL A PASSING GA
LLEY THE BODY O
F RAISED LETTER
S HAIL A PASSIN
G GALLEY THE BO
DY OF RAISED LI
TTERS HAIL A PA
SSING GALLEY TH
E BODY OF RAISE
D LITTERS  HAIL
A PASSING GALLE
Y THE BODY OF R
AISED LETTERS H
AIL A PASSING G
ALLEY  THE BODY
OF RAISED LITTE
RS HAIL A PASSI
NG GALLEY THE B
ODY OF RAISED L
```

BY THE SLICE   BY THE CUP

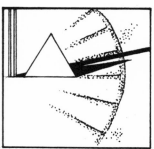

(Puzzling) Intrinsically

Rock breaks scissors

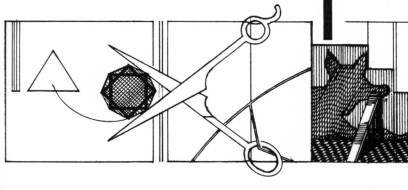

Scissors cuts paper

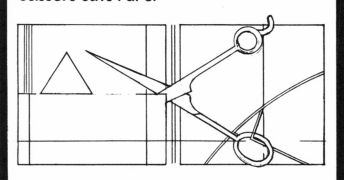

Out came the sun
And dried up all
the rain

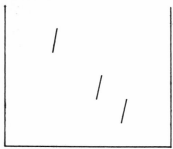

And
The itsy-bitsy spider
climbed up the spout
again.

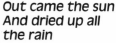
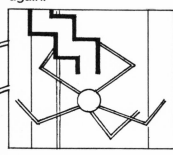

14

Behind the Flat

Caterpult

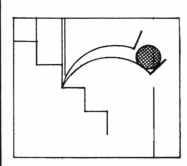

Hanging punctuation

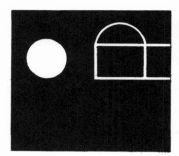

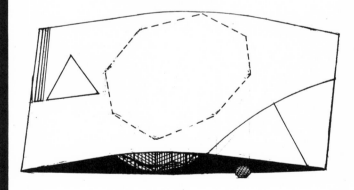

```
ħħħħħħ......
atThePASSINGofA
lEADERtheASSEMB
LEDmournSOLIDLY
atThePASSINGofA
lEADERtheASSEMB
LEDmournSOLIDLY
atThePASSINGofA
lEADERtheASSEMB
LEDmournSOLIDLY
 atThePASSINGof
aLEADERtheASSEM
BLEDmournSOLIDL
Y atThePASSINGo
faLEADERtheASSE
MBLEDmournSOLID
LY atThePASSING
ofaLEADERtheASS
EMBLEDmournSOLI
DLY atThePASSIN
GOfaLEADERtheAS
SEMBLEDmournSOL
```

Let us read deep
And say amend.

Choosing a target
Taking aim

A wide scream

Paper covers rock

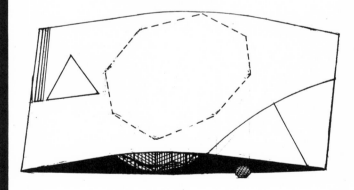

Adagio

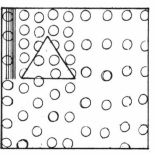

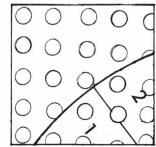

Cocking the Spiral hammer

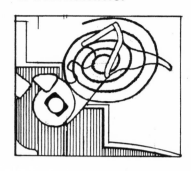

Thoughts are things
Thoughts have wings

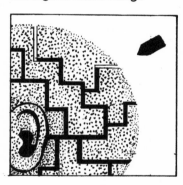

15

Drawn away by litter

All things sweep up.

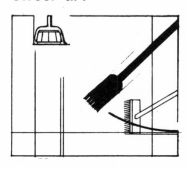

Commuting by site, Taking the chain four stops.

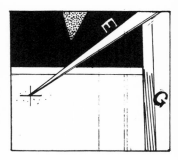

"...watch the closing doors!"

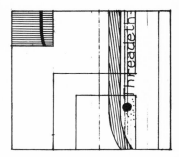

"...watch the closing doors!"

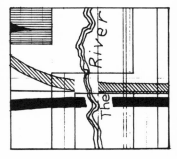

"...watch the closing doors!"

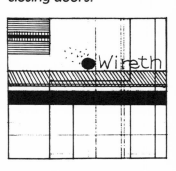

Shuffling
Half empty   Half full

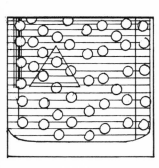 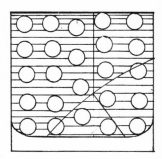

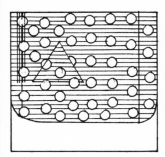 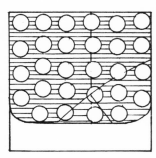

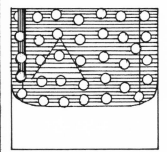 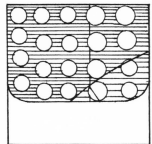

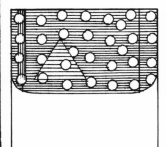 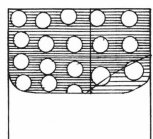

Taking the pulse three beats

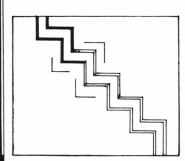

Riverroad
(TWO BY TWO)

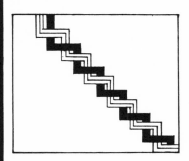

16

By black track

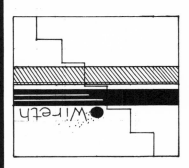

To Drink-of-the-ink and

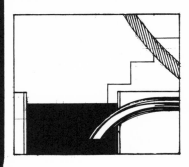

Last stop.
O chamber!
O chambre!
O camera !

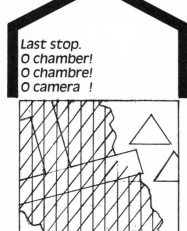

The warmth of evening.
Lying beneath the moonlit flake.

Back to home.

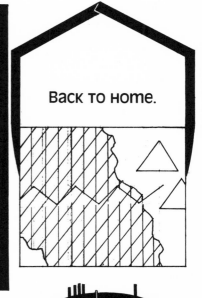

CRYSTAL SPLICE

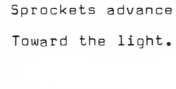

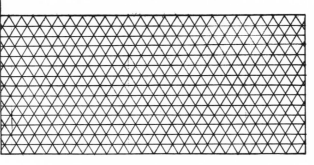

Sprouts spring

Trouts spawn

Sprockets advance

Toward the light.

Stirring

Deep in wells

Stylus points

Inscribed by night.

The trio wails in assent

Five bar blind

Three shades
Three steps

Eye sign

The pair confers

In descent

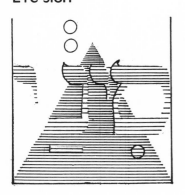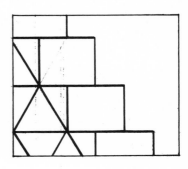

One receives
(WADING)

MIDDLE SIGN

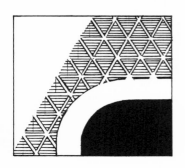

Descend!

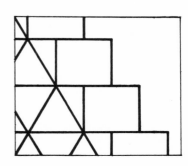

WAITING ON THE CORNERSTONE

DESCENDANT AT THE CORNERSTONE

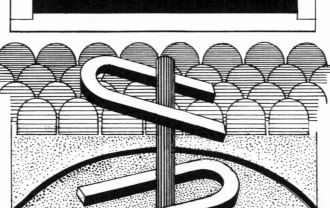

EXODUS: XXXII

17 And when Joshua heard the noise of the people as they shouted, he said unto Moses, There is a noise of war in the camp.

18 And he said, It is not the voice of them that shout for mastery, neither is it the voice of them that cry for being overcome: but the noise of them that sing do I hear.

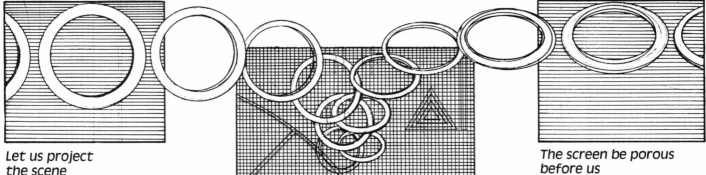

Let us project the scene as seen.

The screen be porous before us between us.

A Round,
THE GOLDEN:

**MOUSE/CALF
HOUSE/HIVE
DRUM/TABLE
HORN/CUP
LEAF/FLAME**

TESTIMONY

**APPLE/EGG/MOON
BREAD/BOOK/RUNE
POLE/GATE
HILL/SLIDE
DREAM/CIRCUS**

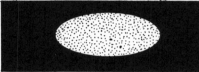

Three Blind mice
Three Blind knights
See how they run
Shadows of one
They all trip after
The former half
Who could often, to serve
Pass for wheat or for chaff
Did you ever stitch
Such a knot in your calf?
Through these blind nights

These resonant nights
These resonant nights
Sea howls they rush
Sea hounds they rust
They all drain after

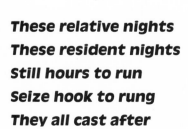

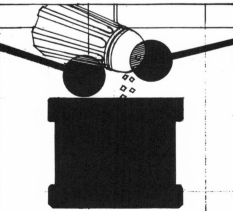

These relative nights
These resident nights
Still hours to run
Seize hook to rung
They all cast after

These attempts to speak
These attempts to speak
See round they run
Drunk by the tongue
They all roll after
The former's words

These traveled ropes
These given roads
Steer as they wind
Shift as they bend
They all turn after
The former sight
Which could
Muddle the trail
Topple the pail
Murder the tale
Through a curving night
Each, however the source
Each, whoever aside
Each, whatever you say
Serves their slice of advice
Eats their size of the ripe
And so treads light
And so stays late

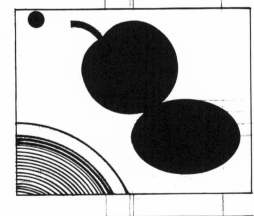

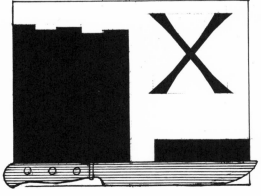

These behind nights
Deeply mined nights
Shape how they run
Sift through the hum
They all trail after
The former's wake

Those bound in flight
Those born in flight
From whom they run
To whom they run
They all dance after
The fertile beat
Which could offer up tolls
Fill up the bowls
Sweeten the goals
Without fail, to repeat
Without fear, to repeat

20

Three blinking lights
Three blinking lights
Stop, wait and go
Stop, wait and go
They all fall after
A sequence of weight
Which blurs past details
At the turn of each take
Which echoes return
At the switch of each fate
Which trips first concerns
At the close of each race
Did you ever leap past
The time and the rate
The tide of the date
The height of the gate
By

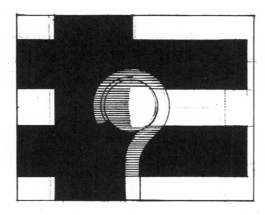

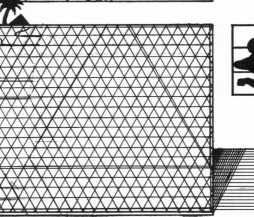

Three blind twice
Three blind twice

These whispering nights
These choral nights
Sing staggered rhymes
Send brittle lines
That all call after

These blinking lights
These sibling minds
There belied my eyes
There devise my eyes
There divide my eyes
There behind my eyes
We all dream under
The resting beat
We all hear over
The ticking beat
The drip
And drip
And drip

21

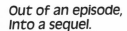

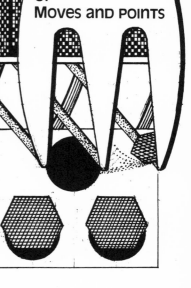

Out of an episode,
Into a sequel.

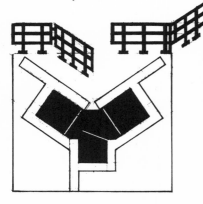

THE
THIRD PERSON
TAKES A STAND

2

Out of the crib,
And into the craft.

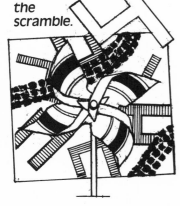

He dressing frantically, leaves for work.
She sleeping heavily, gains more time.
she lying bundled in bears, begins to talk turkey.

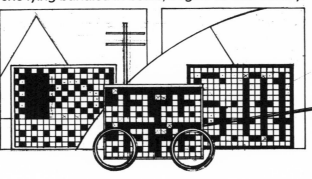

KNOTS
AND STRINGS

Out of the crawl,
And into
the
scramble.

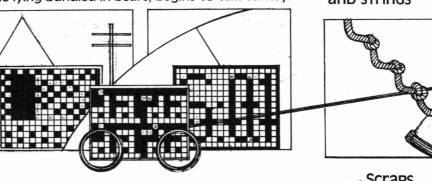

Scraps
AND
CAPS

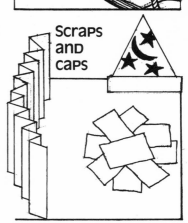

22

Out of the touch,
And into the toss.

Oracular

(SPEAK)

dat

dat dat dat dat dat dat dat dat dat dat dat

dat....

WHO IS SHE?
Drawn to familiars
A kiss on the mirror.

OF TRICKS AND TRUMPS
THE RECORD IS NEARLY RUN

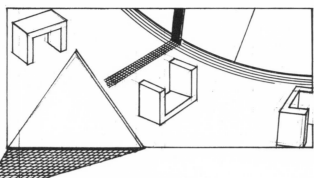

To plant in the East:
A willowy cap with
All weather flaps.

WHERE IS SHE?
Combing the kitchen
Banging the pots.

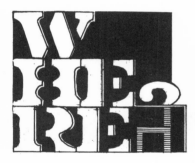

All be seeded!

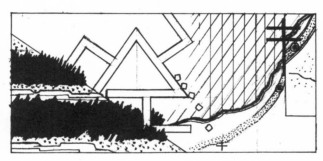

To play in the West:
A conical cap of
Spun woven nap.

WHO IS SHE?
Daughter like others
Daughter like none.

"Thou preparest a table before me
in the present..."

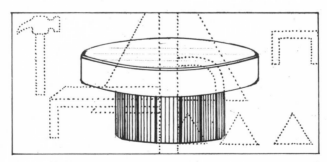

To pace in the North:
A cap both brimmed
and shading.

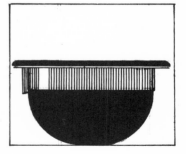

23

WHERE IS SHE?
Prowling the hallways
Chasing the cats.

Second Deal
(TO SECOND GUESS
THE SECOND GUEST)

To place in the South:
A cap both walled
and watching.

WHO IS SHE?
*A being born separate
A child connected.*

(from the North)
*"All I've passed, sampled, piled,
I bid there the same."*

TAKING THE PULSE
FOUR BEATS,
FIVE BEATS,
SIX BEATS.

(from the West)
*"Dat-dat-dat-dat-dis,
ALL MINE!"*

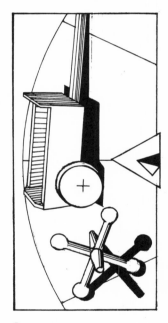

WHERE IS SHE?
*Out in the pasture
Winding the clocks.*

RIVERROBE

STITCHING

WHOOOOOOOOOOOOOO

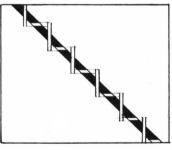

(from the East)
"I'll if asked give'm double."

24

A TALE OF
CLOAK AND TAILOR
FLOOR AND CEILING

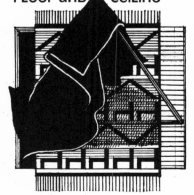

(from the South)
*"Heads up, and hear the speaker out.
I'll waltz them all about."*

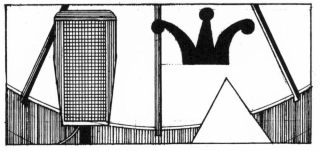

The Game: WHERE CHANGE IS CONSUMED BY HABIT
AND STALKED BY RITUAL.

Cards to the WEST   Cards to the NORTH/Cards to the SOUTH   Cards to the EAST

(A ROPE)

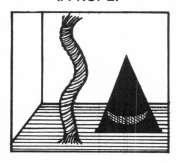

The man upstairs, propelled in faith, begins to take steps.

The man below, distracted in truth, listens from the corner.

I WILL, I AM

THE BIDDING: For the EAST: Something dropped, something named, something lost, something gained.
Hidden in speculation, SOUTH lets the moment pass.
For the WEST, a rope to nowhere, DAT!
Given first cause, NORTH takes the first hand.

1

(A TUBE)

With time, the stepping accelerates, back and forth.

With repetition, the listening focuses, up and across.

YOU ARE

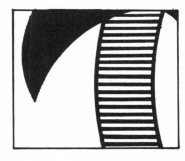

THE BIDDING: NORTH, lost in habit, follows in his own footsteps.
For the second, SOUTH takes notice, defensively.
WEST, unraveled at length, displays a formidable lack of seriousness.
For shifting the blame successfully, EAST wins the second hand.

2

(A ROLL)

Above, holding the pace.

Below, holding in place.

YOU MUST BE
(THEY WILL)

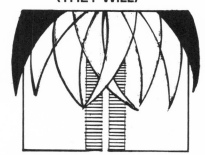

25

THE BIDDING: ALL PASS to their betters. Once around for all concerned.

3

(A HOLE)

The pacing stops suddenly without calculation. The quiet builds slowly.

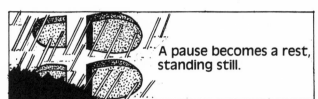

The listening intensifies with anticipation. The tension grows audibly.

WE ARE

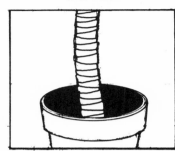

THE BIDDING:
4
NORTH. No calculation?
Planted in definition, EAST stands pat with split intentions.
Under the weight of externals, SOUTH hangs poised in place.
For maintaining the option to come and go, WEST eludes the game and wins the fourth hand.

(A RING)

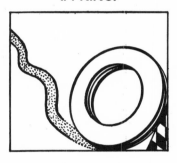

A pause becomes a rest, standing still.

Listening becomes waiting, sitting still.

I AM, I WILL

THE BIDDING:
5
NORTH stands grazed. Overgrown and under led, under lock and creeper.
Left with fresh points of indecision, SOUTH remains suspended.
In the WEST, "ashes, ashes, all fall down!"
EAST, in concert, takes the fifth. A firm solo performance confirming earlier expectations.

(A TOP)

Silence fills the space above, expanding to a hum.

Quiet remains in place, seated in the corner.

YOU MIGHT BE

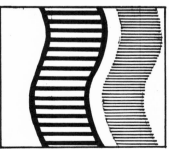

26

THE BIDDING:
6
Disconnected, NORTH yields to the drift. Half empty, half full.
EAST slides on shifting hopes. A reservation for one.
SOUTH, in camera, folds early, wrapped in self-reflection.
WEST wins the sixth. All things said and meant, spin like a top.

(SPRING)

 The pacer still stands in the middle of the room.

The listener, no longer listening, shifts to another corner.

WE WILL

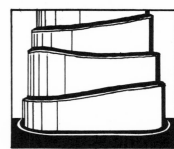

THE BIDDING:

7

NORTH holds, anchored to the past with the game at sixes and sevens.
EAST. We will, hopefully.
WEST balks at being directed; in default for leaping in place.
Finally, stroked by ambivalence, habit rolls over, bringing the form of the new. SOUTH takes the 7th.

(BOTTLE)

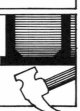 The pacer, feeling the shift, takes a single cautious step and holds.

The step taps the memory. The listener awakened, returns to his vigil.

I AM, I WILL

THE BIDDING:

8

EAST, in good company, but no match for the sentiments of the past.
In the SOUTH. A moment of optimism, but, one tap too many?
WEST on retreat, unapproachable in the corner.
With affection, a return to former days. NORTH takes the eighth hand.

(PENCILS)

 The pacer, with familiarity, renews his stepping.

The listener, with familiarity, renews his listening.

YOU COULD BE (THEY WILL)

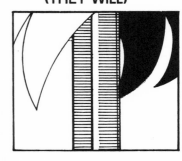

THE BIDDING:

9

Comfort before content. NORTH trips on in routine fashion.
A lack of cards on the table. EAST holds close with reserve.
A return to the internal dialogue. SOUTH runs out of touch.
Riding intricate figures, WEST regains the spotlight and the ninth hand.

(BEADS)

The pacing continues as before.

The listening continues as before.

WE ARE

THE BIDDING: ALL PASS to their favorites. Once more for all concerns.

10

(WHEELS)

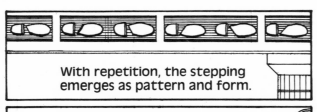

With repetition, the stepping emerges as pattern and form.

With time, the sound recedes as background and rhythm.

YOU ARE, YOU ARE

THE BIDDING: The dance becomes history. NORTH steps away, above the conflict.
A blank verse for the SOUTH: "With washed attention, he lost the place."
WEST rolls past, without hesitation, undisturbed by early moves.
Facing home, EAST confronts the present and gains the 11th hand.

11

(BEAR)

Breaking the pattern, the pacer finds the door.

Sitting unaffected, the listener finds his foot.

IT SHOULD BE (YOU SHOULD BE)

28

THE BIDDING: EAST (She) looking forward, gains more time.
In the end, distracted on faith, SOUTH looks on better days.
WEST (she) sitting tired with bears, begins to lose patience.
Given a way out, NORTH has the last word.

12

WHY?

...Because having conducted the ultimate chorus of cycling and circling, without climax, crescendo or relief, I am compelled, at last, to face the motion, stop the music, to make my point...A point of reference without which there would be no sense of having come so far and accumulated so much. The period that makes the sentence, commutes the term, notes in passing, the way around the wall. But first, before the rest, there must be a pileup, head on, first to last, end to end, a quick accounting of the parts and measuring of the distance leading to the point of present departure.

(SMOKE)

At last, above, the pacer returns with a chair...but

At first, tapping is heard in the room below...then

I WILL, I AM

THE CHEESE STANDS ALONE

The Third Audition
THE LAMENTER

O cow are you?
Cow in the field
Staring straight
Chews intently
Downing her lot
To be milked reverently.
After dinner
Out to graze
Whether's clear
Pass the praise.
O, cow are you?
O, cow are we?
SHEEP!

"Mr. East Gave a Feast,"
Before The Altar Of The Self

Of Means And Tools And Vantage Points

(At sunset)

30

"Mr. North, Laid The Cloth;" On Walls, Screens And

THE REFRAIN:
One cloth, one cloth,
One cut from the same cloth.

THE CHEESE STANDS AT HOME

Mirrored Halls, The Insides Of A Portable Shelter

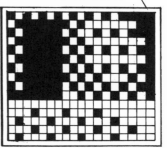

First came,
you don't expect me
to accept this
(refrain)

Then came right or wrong,
what's more no less
(refrain)

Then came this or that,
as this sometimes happens
(refrain)

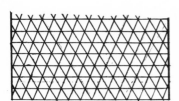

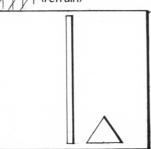

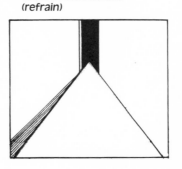

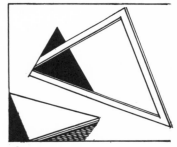

Then came his nerve
(refrain)

Then came the other
(refrain)

Then came, so he said:
(refrain)

Then came,
be specific
(refrain)

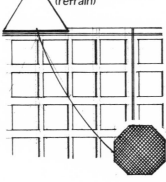

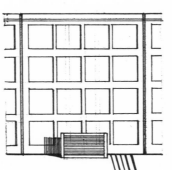

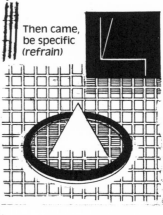

Then came, have patience
(refrain)

Then came what fell flat
and called it even
(refrain)

Then came the time
to mention; to cast
one for the other
(refrain)

(In the snow)
Then dined the replacement
and whined the original,
half empty, half full,
half frozen.
(refrain)

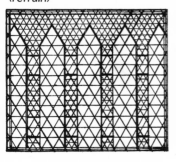

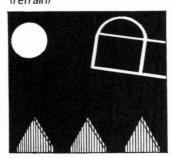

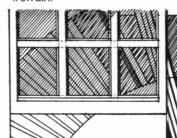

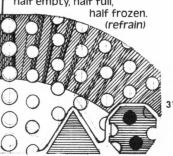

31

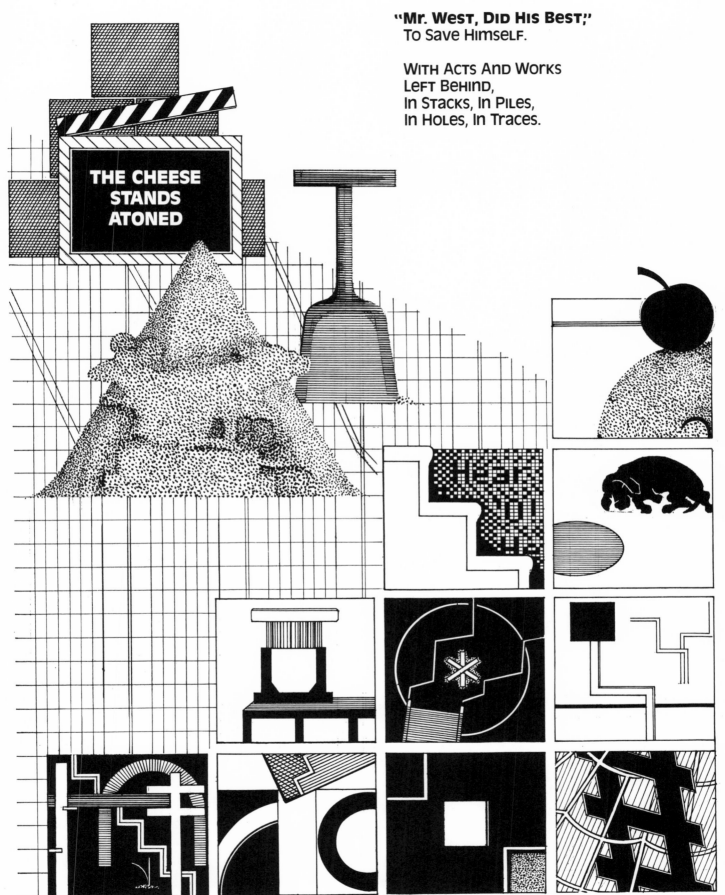

"Mr. West, Did His Best," To Save Himself.

With Acts And Works Left Behind, In Stacks, In Piles, In Holes, In Traces.

THE CHEESE STANDS ATONED

32

**"Mr. South,
Burned His Mouth
With Eating A Cold Potato,"**

Or so he feared.
And his thoughts held close
And he waited.

*Taking the pulse
seven beats*

*Taking the pulse
eight beats*

*Taking the pulse
nine beats*

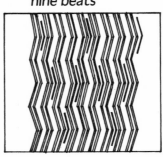

"May the words
of my mouth,
and the meditation
of my heart..."

And so he waited
And so he thought
Until he saw

That as he sat
The more he hoped
The more he looked

And so he walked
And so he danced
And so he sang:

Riverroll

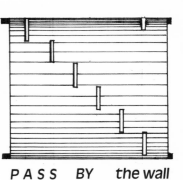

P A S S	*BY*	*the wall*
NOTICE		*the wall*
STARE	*AT*	*the wall*
Then		
M O V E	*TO*	*the wall*
LEAN/	*ON*	*the wall*
BACK	*ALONG*	*the wall*
THINK	*OF*	*the wall*
Then		
PRESS	*TO/*	*the wall*
EAR	*TO*	*the wall*
NOSE	*TO*	*the wall*
FIN - GER		*the wall*
Then		
CLING	*TO*	*the wall*

33

T-A-P - ON the wall
D R A W ON the wall
QUESTION . . . the wall
Then
LET GO the wall

SIT BY the wall
PON - DER the wall
CROUCH BY the wall
Then
WON - DER the wall

SC AL IN G the wall
VAULT ON the wall
STRA DDLE the wall
Then
DREAM ON the wall

S C A NNING the wall
M-A-P OF the wall
THREAD OF the wall
Then
CAST - ING the wall

FALL OFF the wall
SCRAPED BY the wall
SWAYED BY the wall
Then
PASSED BY the wall

PAUSED BY the wall
Then
PASSED BY the wall